Muskegon Area District Library

FIREFIGHTERS
on the Job

By Lee Fitzgerald

Published in 2017 by
KidHaven Publishing Imprint of Greenhaven Publishing LLC
353 3rd Avenue
Suite 255
New York, NY 10010

Copyright © 2017 KidHaven Publishing, an Imprint of Greenhaven Publishing, LLC.

All rights reserved. No part of this book may be reproduced in any form without permission in writing from the publisher, except by a reviewer.

Designer: Deanna Paternostro
Editor: Katie Kawa

Photo credits: Cover, p. 17 Jupiterimages/liquidlibrary/Thinkstock; p. 5 Tyler Olson/Shutterstock.com; p. 7 Tatiana Belova/iStock/Thinkstock; p. 9 Mishella/Shutterstock.com; p. 11 Elnur Amikishiyev/Hemera/Thinkstock; p. 13 monkeybusinessimages/iStock/Thinkstock; p. 15 Monkey Business Images/Monkey Business/Thinkstock; p. 19 rasento/iStock/Thinkstock; p. 21 MattGush/iStock/Thinkstock; p. 23 William Perugini/Shutterstock.com.

Library of Congress Cataloging-in-Publication Data

Names: Fitzgerald, Lee, author.
Title: Firefighters in our community / Lee Fitzgerald.
Description: New York : KidHaven Press, [2017] | Series: Jobs in our
   community | Includes bibliographical references and index.
Identifiers: LCCN 2016036204 (print) | LCCN 2016044077 (ebook) | ISBN
   9781534521414 (pbk.) | ISBN 9781534521421 (6 pack) | ISBN 9781534521438
   (library bound) | ISBN 9781534521445 (E-book)
Subjects: LCSH: Fire extinction–Vocational guidance–Juvenile literature.
Classification: LCC TH9119 .F58 2017 (print) | LCC TH9119 (ebook) | DDC
   363.37023–dc23
LC record available at https://lccn.loc.gov/2016036204

Printed in the United States of America

CPSIA compliance information: Batch #CW17KL: For further information contact Greenhaven Publishing LLC, New York, New York at 1-844-317-7404.

Please visit our website, www.greenhavenpublishing.com. For a free color catalog of all our high-quality books, call toll free 1-844-317-7404 or fax 1-844-317-7405.

CONTENTS

Brave Firefighters. **4**

What They Wear **14**

Fast Fire Trucks **18**

Words to Know **24**

Index **24**

Firefighters work hard to keep us safe. They are very brave!

Firefighters save people from fires.

Firefighters put out fires, too. They use water from a **hose**.

A **ladder** helps firefighters reach high places.

Firefighters also help people who are sick or hurt.

A firefighter wears a **helmet**. It keeps their head safe.

There are special clothes and boots for firefighters, too.

Firefighters drive in a fire truck. Many fire trucks are red.

A fire truck has lights on top. It also has a siren that makes loud noises.

21

Firefighters need to get to work quickly. Fire trucks can go fast!

WORDS TO KNOW

helmet   hose   ladder

INDEX

C
clothes, 16
F
fire truck, 18, 20, 22

S
siren, 20
W
water, 8